JOKER, JOKER, DEUCE

JOKER,
JOKER,
DEUCE

PAUL BEATTY

PENGUIN ◆ POETS

PENGUIN BOOKS
Published by the Penguin Group
Penguin Books USA Inc., 375 Hudson Street,
New York, New York 10014, U.S.A.
Penguin Books Ltd, 27 Wrights Lane,
London W8 5TZ, England
Penguin Books Australia Ltd, Ringwood,
Victoria, Australia
Penguin Books Canada Ltd, 10 Alcorn Avenue,
Toronto, Ontario, Canada M4V 3B2
Penguin Books (N.Z.) Ltd, 182–190 Wairau Road,
Auckland 10, New Zealand

Penguin Books Ltd, Registered Offices:
Harmondsworth, Middlesex, England

First published in Penguin Books 1994

3 5 7 9 10 8 6 4 2

Copyright © Paul Beatty, 1994
All rights reserved

Some of the poems in this book previously appeared in *AGNI, Eyeball, Gathering of the Tribes, Longshot, The Portable Lower Eastside, Slam Poetry,* the *St. Marks Poetry Anthology,* and *West Coast Line.*

Grateful acknowledgment is made for permission to reprint excerpts from the following copyrighted works:
"It Takes Two" by R. Ginyard. © 1988 Protoons, Inc./Hikim Music/ASCAP. Used by permission.
"Float On," words and music by Arnold Ingram, James Mitchell Jr. and Marvin Willis. © Copyright 1977 by Duchess Music Corporation. All rights controlled and administered by MCA Music Publishing, a division of MCA Inc., New York, NY 10019. Used by permission. All rights reserved.
"I Feel the Earth Move" by Carole King. © 1971 Colgems-EMI Music Inc. All rights reserved. International copyright secured. Used by permission.
"Felix the Wonderful Cat" by Winston Sharples. Copyright © 1958 and 1961 by Famous Music Corporation.

LIBRARY OF CONGRESS CATALOGING IN PUBLICATION DATA
Beatty, Paul.
Joker, joker, deuce / Paul Beatty.
p.   cm.
ISBN 0 14 05.8723 3
I. Title.
PS3552.E19J65   1994
811'.54—dc20   93–31264
Printed in the United States of America
Set in Electra
Designed by Katy Riegel

This book is dedicated to my families, both biological:
Ma, Anna, Sharon, Grandma, Ainka;
and extended:
the Chacons, the Keatons, the 46 Crew, and Toi Russell.
Later.

ACKNOWLEDGMENTS

A special thanks to Bobby Ward, Joe Mackenzie, Carlos Colon, Mona Phillips, Jamahl Carter, Love and Rockets (the comic book), and Chow Yun-Fat.

CONTENTS

JOKER, JOKER, DEUCE

At Ease

every morning roundabout nine
the east 2nd street
red fire engines whine

     a shrill drill sergeant
     rousting my mind

             its time to rise and shine   shine
  in the east village
  another dollar draft recruit
     boot camp saloon sambo
         a genesee on tap dancin hambone poet

bivouacs in the groovy lower east side barracks
makin friends wid homespun poet pundit bums
constantly recitin jack kerouac

and for fun i attend
allnight outdoor open mikes
free readings about real people
who seem so lifelike

    last night i bought a stolen bike
    a freewheel three speed
    grew a goatee

camped out on avenue B
and for a change in perspective
went to   A Retrospective of Scatological Abstraction:
           from Popeye to Gillespie

           skeeter ta rebop rap pap debose
                 debang
                 deboom

1

                                        i yam what i yam
                                and thats all that i yam
b'diddly bop repetitious rot
dont forget to stop at my seddity sop co-op
                                listen to my loizada
                                        lambada
                                        tostada
cholesterol-free blah blah blah poppycock

                                        salt free nuts
                                        salt free nuts

i just kickback n watch
black combat boots
move thru an east village tour of duty
                                an in unison death march
                                        to the cadence
of the ultra cool

hop hop who
hut-hop hep who
hut-hop hep who
hut-hop het who
                eeney meany miney moe
                lets go back and write some more

i admit theres an urge
to merge ginsbergs
ice age incantations
with some inspired spitfire monk vibes

                        but no tai chi for me "g"
                        nix on the tye dye

        wont hindu my blues nor
                        tofu my soulfood

                                                        2

im gonna be
    the bulimic bohemian

                eatin up my people
                then purgin their regurgitated words
                on the page
                            and the poems
                        become self made
                little icarus birds
        immaculately hatched
from the multicultural nest eggs
of the east village and west l.a.
                    born to sing lyric segues
            while caged
whats the   latin
          scientific
             slave name
for pretty peacocks
      whose feathers span the flesh spectrum
                but are stuck on with wax
it looks nice
but can it fly

      look up in the sky
      itsa bat
      itsa crow
  no its supernigger / indian / chicano / womanist / gay / asian everything

able to fly through the peephole
in the white medias ozone
          talk proper on the phone and act ethnic at home

y know
its like multiculturalisms
the lefts right guard
of truth justice and the american way

                         a spray-on deodorant
                      against the stench of isms
                         Contents under
                         extreme pressure.
                         May explode.

i understand the effort to prevent skin cancer
by removin epithets and fluorocarbons from the history texts

but multiculturalisms
sunblock jargon
                doesnt protect
                against big brother sun rays
                on days when niggas went to the beach and wore socks

to cover up the lack of respect for the blackfeet

    not the indians
                        but the crusty lizard skin
                        two inch thick toenailed
                           curled hammertoes
            knuckled corns *my soul is rested* on

never heard anyone
other than
a black man
utter these words   *man she got some pretty feet*

dont nobody appreciate feet
like we do

        i fell in love with my second grade teachers feet
        her toes smooth n flat   her insteps were all that
        i would drop my pencil a lot
        to watch her wiggle her little piggies under the desk

4

we used to stay after school
to sneak around and smell her shoes
and this little piggy ran all the way home

what you learn in school today

bout how columbus
landed in cuba stuck a flag in the ground
how neil armstrong landed on the moon and stuck a flag in the ground
how rick rubin landed in rap and stuck a flag in the sound

hey you all look what i found

the east village
a human garden   a botanical class menagerie
with its own avant-garde beatnik color guard

that when asked to
present the colors of their flag
                              they go   *white and ummm*
                                        bob kaufmann aaaand lets see uhhhh
                                        oh yeah the angry guy

hey leroi

i joined this peoples army
to seek that quintessential beat freedom
that only white boys seem to achieve

the rest of us
still dream about being so casual
being able to act up
with that bill murray i dont give a fuck   boom shaka laka
                                           boom shaka laka
                                           chief house rocker attitude

hey dude care to smoke a bowl   no regrets hold your breath

don't smoke buddha
cant stand sess
its takes two to make-ah thing go right

so i force a discourse
    wid corporal gregory corso
    his pissed on disciples fix bayonets
    point their self righteous rifles   at my writing

dont get upset but
              why dont you [blacks and other oppressed etc.]
              write more universally

does that mean write more white
drink tea in the morning
write about flowers n lust and poeticize the dust in the light rays

        dont pull my daisy

but like paul revere said
at end of his midnight ride   whoa

it never ceases to amaze me
that whenever these jazz crazed
              surly black berets
              police the proud grounds
              of their past
      they always
mention diane diprima last

        boom shaka laka
        boom shaka laka
        thats the fact jack

     i've heard   elvis donny hathaway
     and roberta flack rap about the ghetto

but in the village
        i can peruse stacks n stacks
        of used and overdue library books

rows n rows
        of mad magazine paperbacks
like Al Jaffee's   Snappy Answers
        to Stupid Questions

How does it feel to read in front of so many white people?

snappy answer #1: the tompkins sq. park zoo closes at 1:00am
snappy answer #2: *i feel the earth move under my feet*
        i feel the sky tumblin down
snappy answer #3: sometimes i feel like othello in the last act
        desdemona is thru
        and now usin modern medieval seppuku
        heez fixin to spill his noble guts to the public

    Soft you; a word or two before you go.
    I have done the state some service and they know't;
    . . . Speak of me as I am: nothing extenuate, . . .
    you must speak
    Of one that loved not wisely, but too well; . . .   340
    I took —by th'throat the . . . dog
    And smote him thus.   350

why you stabbeded my brother in the back
i be got no weapon

doin the hollywood shuffle
here in alphabet city
where the contradictions are so deep
you got
        white supremacists
        datin *black chicks*

where the tattooed unclenched fists of anarchists
talk bout if they had money
theyd start the revolution

when if theyd redeem
all the pop bottles
                    they toss at the cops
                    they could at least leaflet
                    all the way to avenue D

but paulo friere multiculturalism and foucault
and the highbrow *whats wrong with the world*
handbilled and postered so and so
dont go into the projects

cuz thats where the for real
dispossessed pink slipped guerrillas in the mist stay at
hangin around   brass monkeys on the buzzards back

and in the middle of my rant
the man said
lighten up jack
straighten up and fly right
cool out and add a white boy to your jazz collection

so i attached gerry mulligans
hook n ladder long-ass sax
fire engine red hair to my wake up solo
this mornin i feel like
a black sideman playin poetic trumpet

                              my my aint that sumpthin

a literary bojangles
inna military band
playin taps

red black n greens at half-mast
his bitterness iz dead

while uptowns fife n thumb drum corps
separates the trapezoids from the squares
           the raw from the done

                   i polish up my buttons n buckles

                   check out my reflection

                   fakin the funk

                   im ready for inspection
lace up my doc martens
and im marchin

hut-hop hop hop het-who
hut-hop hep who
lookin' good   lookin' good
                    lookin' good like you should

Why That Abbott and Costello Vaudeville Mess Never Worked with Black People

who's on first?
i dont know, your mama

That's Not in My Job Description

despite that i overslept
and set a guinness book world record for coming in late
its still time for me to take my 15 minute break

pull off my sweater vest
talking shit

cross my sneakers on the desk
threaten to call my union rep
if these fools

                        dont stop lookin at me crazy
                        whisperin lazy
                        under their breath

but during my siesta
i eavesdrop on societys best

                    imagine im a distinguished ethnographer

on the black pbs
talkin with a british lisp
in front of a bookshelf

welcome to *In Search of*
today we pursue The Elusive True Nature of Whitey

                            notice as
                            our cameras
                            zoom in on

a pin-striped pack of business school well groomed brooks brother
    smoothies
encamped around a water cooler   jostling for room in their natural
    habitat

wiping dunkin donut crumbs off their jackets and engaged in debates
on hot topics
such as:

    nuclear waste the china syndrome
    alternative methods of heating their homes

                         and right before

          the herd starts to roam

    the menfolk take part in the ritual
    shooting of the styrofoam cups into the trash basket

if they make it
they dance around like
they just saved the world

headin my way
lookin for some dap

so i try to look busy
which im good at

start rustlin charts
construct some new paper clip art
chew on a pen cap   as if   im seriously studying my messenger map

hmmmm   did you know that main street runs perpendicular to beech
             and parallel with elm for exactly 1 and seven/eighteenths of
                a mile
             before it intersects with west crest
             well blow me down

i aint got time to mope
worryin aloud about
how imma cope wid radioactive isotopes and mushroom clouds

        when its me myself
                            thats about to explode

an overloaded low level gung-ho ah-so nigro rickshaw coolie
the company dr. doolittles thought they knew me
i talk to the animals como se llama   push-me-pull-me

bowin n kowtowin
eatin crow
holdin my tongue
hands clung so tightly to the bottom rung
cant even reach for the glass ceiling

                    my feet planted in corporate dung

      growing roots
                    in the ground zero
                                        terra firma
                    of affirmative
      daily inaction

                    copy xerox mop remember the blue ones go on top
                    shred fedex the checks press the red button next
                    fax wax collapse the green mail sacks go to jack

right after i put my year-end evaluation
in the management trainee mailbox

one of them fresh out of college cookie cutter fuckers
invites me to meet the buddies for drinks at mcgillicuddy's

i only wanted a nine to five
that classified didnt say nothin bout havin to socialize

now this wage slave
is t-minus nine heinekens from critical mass

me and a few hoogie white democrats
drinking after work rolling rocks
smoking marlboros out the box

all you can do is wait for the chain reaction show of ass

when one of em
looks me in the eye

                    and decides
                              to say something to the colored guy
its
all systems go
the white folks start actin like they know

                hey bro er uh bro-ham
                i happen to be a big rap fan
                went to see ice cube and michel'le
                at the hollywood palladium
                and i was the only white person in the place
                aint i soul brother

there must have been another workshop on how to handle your
     support staff
which in this craft is a euphemism for niggers n spics

itsa trip
watching a one-sided will to unite

if i could get a word in edgewise   i wouldnt
                                      since im with my boss
                                      and dont want to get fired
                    all i can do is sigh
                                      too chicken to pay the price

as they get excited
giddy from overexercising their rights

my dad owns a liquor store in the inner city   so i know how you feel

ive read toni morrisons beloved twice
and even though i still didnt get it the second time   shes just so real

i believe that spike is truly five for five
no no you dont understand   i really want to be like mike

or maybe a harlem globetrotter
its my dream to send my daughter to spelman
where can she get a checkup for sickle cell
whats the name of your hair gel/pomade
do you use a depilatory when you shave
how can i join the crips
just *what is hip*
i know its after the fact but i dont think king shouldve called for calm
i wanna be a minister in the nation of islam
isnt so and so such an uncle tom

when theyre through
they pat themselves on the back
and quote jesse jackson

we have to start on the front end of head start and day care
not on the back end of prison and welfare

keepin hope alive
i buy the next round

wonderin how it would sound if i changed my name to skip
placed a mike tyson kingsized if i ruled the world chip on my shoulder
went to a joint full of rednecks
put my elbows on the bar cleared my throat and said

becks
then i'd go into my show

did you know i was elected to the senate inna landslide
and i was the only colored man there without a rag in my hand for
polishin brass or shining shoes

or

at last weeks tractor pull i was the only spear chukker
drivin monster pick-ups over a bunch of crushed oldsmobiles

or

i sailed in the americas cup

or

i went to the university of vermont   and rowed crew

or

i grew up in a two room shack in the appalachian mountains picked
    myself up
by the shitkickers went door to door selling berlitz and scripture
    moved to
utah sang soprano on the mormon tabernacle choir married into the
    osmonds
and now i spend my weekends smokin pot with donnie and marie
    reading back
issues of teen beat magazine

or

im included in the canon
im a cardinal in the vatican
im the highest paid player on the boston red sox
i own IBM stock
i play nazi punk rock
i drink coors extra gold by the case

i can say puke with a straight face
i have a seat on wall street
im an LL bean catalogue model
my art is in the metropolitan
i had a major part in a woody allen movie
and i do the broadway casting for tommy tune

but i wouldn't give a shit about nuna dis
if i could just say   im a nigger who has enough room

Dib Dab

smooth as . . .

a baby nicholas brother
tap dancin in a porcelain tub
mr bubble suds
aye que lindo palms filled
with cocoa butter lotion

smooth as . . .

michael jordan
in the middle of his fifth
airborne freeze frame pump fake
a funky millionaire marionette
pissin on physics
his glossy fresh out the pacific
sea lion brown skin limbs
draped in 8th century heian kimono silk

smooth as . . .

sarah vaughan
holdin a note dipped in bronze
spit shined with a lonely bootblacks jukebox drool
buffed with chamois cloth and heartache

smooth as . . .

tap beer after midnight mass

smooth as . . .

wilma rudolph haulin ass through rome
long tennessee tigerbelle strides

walkin down gossamer winged myths
busted shackles in her wake
1960 runaway

smooth as . . .

an eric dolphy jazz workshopped
alto free swingin lead
that lets mingus know
where he can shove that bow
if he dont ease up pluckin pizzicato
over his solo

smooth as . . .

billy dee williams   nevermind

smooth as . . .

lady kung fu
flyin roof to roof
dealing five finger drunken monkey style tiger fisted death
to the imperialist aggressors
spinning heel roundhouse
hong kong backlot snap kick sound effects
a buttlength ponytail
trailing the action with a mind of its own

smooth as . . .

the first latin black korean
national hockey league offensive superstar
center ice crossovers
one hand on the stick
blue line breakaway
blastin a drive high and tight

stick side
red light and siren

smooth as . . .

granddads 30 year old
one sunday a month
white patent leather shoes
ones he wears with his lucky powder blue slacks
when he takes you to the track
santa anita belmont yonkers
gives you two disability dollars a race
and tells you to bet the trifecta
on the horses with the names you like

smooth as . . .

a cab calloway blip blap big band stikkle tat riff
rolling over his process
from front to back
sliding on its knees
down the greased part
of a geechee ghetto trickster in full regalia

smooth as fuck

Annotation of a Funky Breakdown

yo Pooh, . . . scratch compton

whahuchwckhoowckhoowckhoowckhoo COMPTON

No Tag Backs

on the catnip tip
i can feel the spit from my bottom lip
　　　　　　stick to the boys bathroom spliff

hey yo nigguh　　　*take a bigger hit*
　　　　　　　　bell rings and i sit
　　in my silla

trapped in the back of spanish class
tappin my hands and feet
　　　　　　　to the post pot goddamn im fucked up
　　　　　　　purple sinsemilla rote learning echo

repite por favor　favor　　favor
　　hace calor　calor　　calor

　　　　　this mess sounds like
an español round of row row row　row your boat
　　　　　　　　where only the doofus kids spoke
　　　entiendes pablo　blo　blo　　what page are we on

asked mi amiga　　la china in front of me　　¿uh que pagina?
and she hooked me up with an hace frío　　frío　　frío

　　and i shivered
　　in the thought that last night the freed seals
　　who normally squawk up n down
　　　　　　　　　the frozen tundra
of my block
　　　　　watched in silence
balancin beach balls of anger on their noses

　　　　as animal trainers in badges
　　　　slaved my music

hiphop assume the position
and on the downbeat the beatdown into submission

pie-yow
        tag   nigger
            if you see a nigger then slap that nigger

whap

i watched the flies take off and land
on the runway lacerations the strap left behind

wont be needin a redcap to carry my baggage
looks like my flight to the promiseland has been delayed

now boarding
a one-way FM daydream diatribe
that plays music that i like but would never buy

bye bye i wish america die
drove my moped to the old heads
but the old head was high
them new jacks was drinkin cisco n colt 45
singin thisll be the day that i die

            don mclean is not exactly my speed
            so at lunch
            i hocked my walkman
            and bought this comic book
            i got scrunched
between lecciones nueve y diez of my *sol y sombra* text

        its all about how
        this jewish india inked maus and his father
        coped with the holocaust in monthly doses

uh-oh im busted
mi profesora is coughin
chalk on her face

                and givin me the *whaaaaa waa*
          waa whaaaaaa
             whaaa
                whaaaaan charlie brown lecture
    cuz im supposed
        to be
        conjugatin the verb cantar
        not readin about auschwitz
aint thata bitch

yo canto so fuckin what you nat king cole or somethin
tu cantas you aint my boss   i dont have to sing no more
                jus pick the cotton

or have you forgotten
nosotros cantamos   we singin so loud

    i almost didnt hear
    balloon shaped shouts of the
    survivor maus point out

that the feline nazi cops

        put the krazy kat
        krystallnacht cartoon kibosh on hiphop
with forty five
commercial free
minutes of continuous nonstop nightstick gnip gnop

        see why heathcliffs luftwaffes
           gnipping
          garfields wehrmachts
           gnopping

this nasty
two step poker faced goose step
that kicked the deuces are wild deuces are kept zest
                out the pez dispenser
                                of uncensored expression

till a candycoated tongue that once drunk from
underground streams of breakbeats

                on jaw trips that spelunked
                into the memorybank depths of exploratory cave funk

        is now twisted
                drippin
                        sugarfree spittle
                        in the middle
                        of a housing project lobby

checkout the SS cheshire cat
crackin up at raps last dance

you'll laugh so hard
        your sides will ache
                your heart will go pitter pat

                        watchin felix
                        the wonderful cat

open his music critic bag of tricks
and host the autopsy on hiphops body

i am now removing
                the rusty wheels of steel
                so molded
                        corroded
that the motor booty seems to have exploded

                    also noted is that the sacroiliac is broken

and the token grammy award
is scratched from all the glass shrapnel
dispatched when rap shattered the window of radio access

and despite
lack of evidence
                    doc felix ruled the assassination
                    of a *paragraph*
                              president a suicide

citing the fact that
even though einstein knew   energy = an emcee squared

even he was not prepared to ride his bike
through the stupid stage show of the third reich

                              here go the mike psych
                              master race
                              permanently turnin down
                              the bass

        and all thats left is this
strange
                    purina cat chow
                         chowchow chow
meow mix of copasetic midrange n rhetoric treble
that blitzkriegs
old school
schoolroom history
                    boom boom boom
                    the civil war was fought for who
                         oh yeah
                         and yall fought world war II for the jews

skippin the pop quiz
the refugee children of rap
                new jack n jill swing
went on about their biz

and prepared for the funeral
        by placin ma raineys shoes
                on the pulpy mishigas remnants of hiphop

princess tam tam
count basies big band
the bar keys and the mythical bessie smith carried the casket

and when the harlem renaissance
bent down to kiss the swollen lips of todays race music

                tears smeared
                the cosmetics
                of the new black aesthetic

                        but this necrophilia swap of spit
                        with the oral tradition

        was the literary CPR
        needed to emergency jumpstart hiphops heart

rampart this is squad 51
we have a few
                recharged zombies of the livin blues

        blind lemon jeffersonian niggas with attitudes part II

        bum rushin the louvre   paintin tunes in the dark

fuck the french
                        fuck mona lisa and her crew

and if you disapprove of me
not knowin the ontology of the white mans muse

well fuck you too

cause this music
is a color struck dermatologists dream
a hand cream
smoove enough to soften
this black skin white masquerade
frantz fanonmena escapade that porcelana lovesongs
make oppression fade away

> *if lovin you is wrong*
> *i dont wanna be right*
> back where i started from
> in the back of the bus
> listenin to the engine hum   we shall overcome

its hiphops job to knockout pop
outbox radio stars that try to drown out hatred
with acoustic guitars

> and harmonies
> written on paper canvases
> where the rhythmless dance

> to a pseudo groove that crosses over imaginary schisms

we're all human beings bullshit
that should be givens
not revelations
> *people are people*
> *especially you all i mean the unequal*

there go rap
kizzickin dazzle mathematics

distance traveled = time divided by
                      _____

                      the speed of the beat

all the gestapo in house go hoooooooo
all the crack babies go aaaaaooooooowwwww

        did you ever notice
how   dances reflect the sign of the times
say its
nineteen eightynine
the beats have slowed down
        and spellbound en tre pre neur'i al black capitalists
                    silkscreen malcolm x on crew neck t shirts
                        for nubian humans

    buy any
jeans necessary

shrink-to-fit *poverty of ideology*
is 100% cotton or have you forgotten
the clorox lyrics to dixie
still bleach the teachings
and when colors bleed
the fight for your rights begins anew

hiphop rings the bell
for round 2
    you get up off your stool
                            doin that dance the runnin man
                swingin your hands perpendicular to the ground
feet sweepin the floor
in an exaggerated muhammad ali
skip stop gesticular tantrum of muscle

            shufflin between the snare drum

                                        and the inherent urge to hustle

goddamn this music feeds
acme iron pellet fake bird seed
to road runners with world class speed

who cant escape
the magnetic pull of wile e. coyotes bullshit dj super genius

in 1886 you should have seen us
we had just broke out of the reconstruction cocoon
so reborn
        butterfly mcqueens
                with somethin to prove
                beyond sambo buffoonery

we invented the cakewalk
a dance
                where even if
                you was sharecroppin in clodhoppers
                gettin county checks
                        it looked like you was dancin
                        in your sunday best

liftin your knees
to your puffed up chest   a hand on your hip

                                and now with your hip on hand

you can digitally sample
any decade on wax

                        twistin through the leather jacketed fifties
                        onna thumb suckin tonal time trip

it hit me

i began to   *wonder wonder*
if the rhythm stick is a psychological whip
that makes body rockin licorice sticks

                              put up with
                              sexist homophobic lyrics
                              just to be hip

theres a place i know where the hipsters go
called bedrock twist twist

the musics in fifth
so why cakewalk over the psychology of oppression
when you can run the motherfucker over

hiphop goes bronco
four wheelin over the bump
                  runnin over the funky chicken in the road
excuse me   do i have treadmarks on my soul
                  if you didnt you wouldnt be in here

                              tradin cigarettes with james brown
                  makin big hits
out of tidbits of soul

                  soon at the end of poems
                  credits not heads will roll

this is dedicated to the one eyed love
the cycloptic papa of hiphop
the uncle wannabe "commie" paul robeson

first to boast
        that he aint no broken down

                  conduit

                              field nigga

river of spit

for you to sail down in your popsicle stick ships
flippin through the gq cosmopolitan fashion glamor
of being
down
with the downtrodden
from
harlem to weisbaden

lickin freedom off
the fourth of july bombpop

                              ooohhhhin and aaahhhhin
                    off aurora borealis fireworks
              that burst from plug-in drums

                                        if you was really with it
                                        youd realize these electric riffs
                                        signal a second coming

where the earths no longer fully jockin god
and the anti-christ holds a mike
up front
smokin blunts with an allen funt mean streak

pullin up to armless people in the street
talkin bout
              "pardon me, but do you have the time?"

oh you laugh
eatin two pieces of chicken and a biscuit
finger lickin good and all that shit

but its hiphop that reminds you
that theres old folks eatin kibbles n bits

and if eleanor bumpurs was at the table
sheed be suckin the grease off her wrists

her shotgunned fingers on the floor
pointin out that
hiphop is a politically economically amputeed peoples fist

gettin paid cuz
                    the tills are alive with the sound of music
    and if your *crisis of the negro intellectual*
harold crusian shit dont talk to the party

                              im afraid the people cant use it

Sitting on Other People's Cars

this mingus CD
reminds you of me

our friendship workshop
where nat hentoffian gizzard driven
record jacket criticism rhythms
trickled from the starsky n hutch spinout swirl

                                    in the crown of yo head
                        ran down
                        your back
            with the bumpidy syncopation

            of a bestfriends knuckle
rubbin up and down your spine

till some drummers high hat tapped
the side of your neck

did you get the chills
                        yeah kinda

twenty some odd years old
and i wanted to call your mother

                ask her
                if you could spend the night
                writing on my back

could never tell the difference between
a small kay and an h

                    well sometimes i could tell
                        i would just say i couldnt
                            so you would have to write it again

our compositions
                            were secret missions
                            me on flashlight
                                        you on bow n arrow

and the apple jack sweetened milk
completed the triptych riffs
that kissed us off

into our solo careers   and   the reverb of the mingus years
that im just now hearin   still give me the chills

Verbal Mugging

this is a performance piece
a recitation of woe
that begins with my head bowed
and my eyes closed

either im asleep
or this poem must be deep

i start by speaking real slow and succinct
my diction sittin in a rocking chair
weaving narrated stage histrionics to the page

          needle and tongue click

    a crossover stitch
    that knits the written
              with the bullshit
                told at quittin time

now i pretend to light a cornpipe
and from memory recite
a story of folklore that if it were true i would rather forget

during act II

my face goes solemn and sallow
it seems we've come to the part
where all hope is lost

        heres when
           i make the sign of the cross

give thanks to an *extensive theatrical background*
that allows me to pretentiously
drop to one knee

        so that any fool could see
        that whatever im talking about
        involves some method acting pleas for freedom

performance poetry to go
biodegradable relatedness
you put your elbows on the table
rest your chin on your rodin brass hand
and you dont have to think

cause i illustrate my words
with some cheesy rip-off diana ross and four tops hand gestures
now dressed in mink and rhinestone leisure suit pink
my poem works an imaginary hoe
a slave to a rhythm so real

you can almost hear the refrains of

                "please let my people go"

        spin out the fields
        with a basso so profundo
        you can almos' feel

                the pat of patronization
                on top yo' head

maybe youve noticed
ive lapsed into a southern drawl
and when i say we that means yawl

the reader at one with the bleeder
isnt that how the gentiles learn to feel jesus

clenchin both my fists for emphasis
i clutch them to my chest
to show that you n me together and separate
feel the oppression of every person who's ever
been shot at spat on and shat upon

                    pigs christened
                    in a backwoods baptismal
                    together we are cleansed

wallowing in the muddled dirt wrongs
done to someone else

a pause   and i lower my voice a couple of octaves
             and project so that you can hear me way in the back

i do this in order to convey a poetic warmth
that crackles on the burning memories of fireside chats
with long since dead   grandpop fred
                aunt teddy
        big daddy kane and miss jane pittman

gingerly my missive sits on the edge of the stage
dangles its feet and proceeds
to shove an earnest down-home tone   right down your throat

as i regale you with cliché and tales of ancestors ive never even known

           i end this oral tome
           drenched in sweat
           wiping away the crocodile tears

of happy endings
in a make believe world
where people speed listen and skim

the poet goes round
makin ends meet
by beatin muthafuckas over the head with sound
bangin tuning forks on minds
lookin for vibrations that dont stop with time

About the Author

to me it used to sound so trite
to carry on
        how some
        corny cockamamie sign from the almighty
        had changed your life

                i used to be a little pyromaniac heathen

right before people got out of the revival meetin
i would soak a bush with lighter fluid
climb up a nearby tree
and right when they walked underneath
i would toss a match into the greenery and set the bush on fire

using the ventriloquist techniques
i acquired by back of the comic book mail order
i'd throw my voice

    "this is god . . . quit your job and kill your kids you sinner you"

sometimes i would bring an eye dropper full of water to the swap meet

when no one was lookin
i would
    go by the table of porcelain virgin mary figurines
    and squirt water on their faces to make it look like they was cryin
    and without fail someone from pomona would notice
    drop to their knees screamin "hail mary full of grace"

i was in therapy for two weeks behind that shit

but you never really know
how some stupid shit will change your life
it was a dumb ol movie poster that helped set my shit right

one night after a small group
grad school seminar
on the process of change and power
i went to a boston beat the clock happy hour

it was
tic toc and you dont stop
                drinkin   vodka shots brain erasers dime beer chasers

left wasted buzzed bent and fuzzy faced

                        didnt know who i was
                        but it was my world
                        walkin the streets
                        whistlin neil sedakas calendar girl

        but it was that brandy
        made me start to twirl
        act all namby pamby
        next thing i know im barry manilow singin mandy

you came and you gave
without takin'
but i sent you away

        sounded so sappy
        made myself lovesick
        why inuh fuck do i stick loneliness down my own throat
        when i know i dont have the sea legs for the love boat

out of dramamine
listing to one side
addicted to tv and bitters
i docked my sinkin ship in front of the art house
shouted   isaac the bartender is my pusherman

and threw up on the coming attraction ad

apologized to the cast
a polite   *excuse me   my bad*
to the black actress
and the three brothers that was rushin her

            wait these is negroes
            what?   no truffaut?

with a torn sheet of the globe
i cleaned my mess off the window

didnt todays horoscope
say

                mars is in the house
                and niggas like us
                are on the cusp of being in vogue
                we bout to get over

ever grow just instantly sober?

that night in front of the nickelodeon theater
i stopped waiting for godot

wiped my mouth and severed the spittle rope
i left tied to a reeking pool of liquefied
burger king whopper with cheese no pickles and no sense of purpose

looked like things was going to be different
luckys no longer yoked to pozzo

me and the crew wuz always talking about change
bout revolution and maybe this movie   *she's gotta have it*

would be in the tradition of
jomo kenyatta   or   sugar ray whippin jake lamotta

and we   the macho male persona non grata

      bided our time till opening night
      by cuttin each others crops
      buggin that the struggle takes so long to rectify

four hundred some odd years of playin mother may i
hell they only played the crusades for uh hundred and ninety five

           how you want it?
           medium long on top   round off the bottom

if i hear one more motherfucker say or-gan-ize
if i had a dime
           let me put a part on the side

its nigger night at this spot called the nine and on the one n two
is dj mike the quantum mechanic from cleveland
he likes to stop the music and the lights
yell—WHOLE HOUSE FREEZE—into the mike
and on cue in the middle of your move
you have to stop what you doin
sometimes you look stupid   sometimes you look cool
cant hear nothin but fools breathin
thinkin about what they goin to do next
for a splitsec you really notice the sweat

on the same old folks
         soaked from fightin ghosts in a strobe light

      we'd leave with our ears ringin
           eatin greasy pizza
           talkin in speeches

  pepperoni? dont you know pepperoni is a hermeneutical hegemony
    of hogwash

a major cog in the plot to triangulate an outbreak of trichinosis
an attempt to whereas inflict porkitis on the minds and bloodlines
      of the black man and wo-man
thereby and thusly bringing us down to a pig styical
socialization process of otherwise porcine consumer bovinity

         just kidding

but everything we did was nigga quid pro quo
if you brought up sigmund freud or hegel
you had to counterbalance the eurolabel with dubois
without sayin how much him and freud looked alike

sat up long nights analyzing the psycho
laid back on a found couch
detailing our dreams
redefining the archetypes to our citified lives
passing the peace pipe
sharing secrets

      promise you wont tell?

         my favorite writer is white

            the GI doughboy who marched across
            the western hemisphere taggin walls and bridges
            with *kilroy was here*

i never could figure
if in the heat of battle his bubbleheaded image
was looking over the lip of life   or   hanging on the edge of a cliff

guess it doesnt matter which   cuz the message was *hang in that shit*

hey its time to split and catch this flick
not going to be any hidden meanings in this motherfucker is it?

only need one ticket
for six niggas in spirit
huddled around the back door kickin it
in anticipation of free admission

one of us
          i wont say who
     was carrying on how the african was never gonna rule
     cause brothers be dickin each other
     not patronizing the arts

                         but *we wuz pooooooooooo*
                              oooooooooo
                              oooooooooo
                              oooooooooo
                              ooooooooooooooor wid 54 o's

     if we had the cash the dough we'd buy black
     least this way we dont pay no sales tax
     so we told him to kiss our butts and cut the crap

popped the metal latch
and crashed the rat race

          carl lewis may set the pace
          stayin in his lane
          wavin' the flag for the usa

                    but lotsa niggas run unattached
                    makin up the staggered start
                    by sneaking into theaters

swaggerin under the cover of the show is startin darkness
the glow of exit signs infrared haze and the
isnt that just typical gaze of liberal boston brahmin

hey if you cant stand the immigrant niggers
practicin the socratic method
by talkin to the screen with their feet on the seats
in the athens of the new world

then put an arm around your lover
watch your back keep an eye on your alpaca knit sweaters and mittens

cuz we're the fuckers born every minute
and the pt barnum egress is over there

having said that we tucked ourselves into a place
where the times wuz changing
in dylanesque
              first or surname retrospect
                              it was kinda like walkin into a room
seeing someone
              getting dressed or undressed
              for the first time   and not have to say excuse me

     popcorn n gummy bears   bon-bons
     taste testin the new wine coolers
                              this movie was on
  high fivin across the aisles
  at stereotypes we didnt mind

it was the first time i had ever experienced cinematic uplift

panty man . . . fake billy dee williams motherfucker . . .

we left the theater pumped as the new born pups
that bounced around that blond kids head in that soda commercial
cept that this blond kid was now inspiration
and we teethed on it
singin   *fifty dollar sneakers and i gots no job*

the little niggers have found sounder
there comes a time when a dog

                         gnaws the hand that feeds it
and contrary to logic

                         there is also an obedience
                         school of thought
a leftover hogmaw
dinner table grandpa dogma

                    that colored people should play dumb
                    to get what they want
     playing dumb
     is a lot like playing dead

theres a list of stupid nigger tricks
you can use to get your wish

        go to the hospital lick your wounds in the emergency room and   *sit*
        play sports and   *sic*
        need a gig   *roll over*   *fetch*   stand on your hind legs and   *beg*

maybe this is why whenever i shake a white cats hand
i feel like im giving paw

nobody had to offer spike a raw piece of meat to get him to speak

and with the bark of the male dogs in the first scene
he walked through the hollywood doggie door
past the newspaper in the kitchen
and took a nasty brooklyn shit
in the middle of the dining room floor

i bought you kids this dog and you promised to take care of it

that disjointed spike lee joint
pushed me to write
sometimes you need an open palmed dig'em smack
on the back of your neck to get you up off your ass

went to see it a second time
with kiphanie lynn tia and nik

and over sunday brunch
eggs mixed with hash and the last two slabs of bacon
we tried to redefine the swine

they said
          good thing spike wuddent naked
i dont think i coulda taken it
                              the movie wasnt about dogs
                              but niggas as pigs

he rapes her and she tries
to go back with his sorry ass

you hip to julie dash   who

i guess forty acres and a mule is a poor folks
start to a revolution

                    i try not to put the cart before the horse
                    my mother used to have to withhold my allowance
                    just to get me to mow the lawn
                    much less plow some fields

but everybodys *talkin' bout a revolution*
including four fab white guys
in skinny ties
whose music nike used to sell tennis shoes pre-spike

just do it
you mean do it to it   no no that wont fly in iowa
if only martin luther king was still alive

             i can see it now   organ music   a choir
he'd be wearing red white and blue gym shoes sayin . . .

          this is mlk
          when im marchin on washington   *yes lord*
          coolin my heels in a birmingham jail
          backpedalin in memphis   *mmmmm hmmmm*
          runnin from german shepherds in selma
          cheatin on my wife in hattiesburg   *yes suh*

     i thank god i wear air integrationists crossover trainers by nike

                              hallelujah

heroes   fall   down   and go boom

sittin in the living room
watchin spike run the bulls in pamplona
usin his smushed in butt to sell levis
a handkerchief wrapped around his head

yo your boy . . . the black cecil b. de millionaire has gone commercial

no he hasnt
see his runnin from the bulls
in the streets of formerly fascist spain
is a visual metaphor for the civil rights era
its symbolic of the masses running from sheriff bull connor

you get it? bulls   bull connor?

just cause spike sells the white mans tennies
and runs around europe like a little rascal king of show biz
dont mean he dont know who he is

                         whos that?

that's buckwheat
he owns a mansion and a yacht
and makes hundreds of thousands of dollars

learn that poem
learn that poem

in the age of celluloid soul
the revolution moves at 24 frames per second
thats too goddamn slow

for the folks
at black literary events
kintecloth and dreadlocks
harvard yardies parked in circles drinking fruit juice

listening to the   angry   young   atomless   black   woman poet
smash adjectives

reading fantastic action-packed stanzas
on how one day
               we will be the people we usta be
                    the people we're supposed to be
                    the people we really are

youre either mau-mau or coward
there is no middle ground

i looked over at my partner
and asked him   *who are you*

he opened his mouth

              and before a sound came out i cut him off

no who are you really

he told me about the day his girlfriend
asked him the same thing
and he drew a cartoon of a little man
walking out of a big ol suit of armor   and said thats me

my niggas deep
big barry manilow fan

i write the songs that make the young girls cry
i write the songs, i write the songs

i imagine the poet at home
writing real fast
her pen circling all the revolutionary bases
with the furious zeal of a ball point babe ruth
in an old 1920s news reel hittin home runs   tippin her cap to no one

sometimes the revolution revolutionizes itself
and you dont get what you expect

shut off the tv and went to see angela davis speak
niggas was geeked   expecting to see   the famed afro of death

a medusa redbone natural the circumference of the sun
filled with grenades and guns
rising burn baby burn
over the horizon of the lectern

and then she entered stage right
with an alternative hairstyle

thickassed light brown dreadlocks

humbolt county bud looking

twisted clumps of hair

                oozin from her skull

she looked so tranquil
everybody looked at each other all quiet
and we thought to ourselves *oh fuck the revolutions dead*

i wanted to pour off the top of my heart in the gutter
and say this is for the motherfuckahs who aint here
and who stopped me on the street the day after askin

what angela say about fannie lou mary mccleod bethune?
what angela say about the revolution?
what she say about *women racism and class?*

          she said what she said   what did you hear she said

i heard she said some things she didnt have to say

          that's right   she said some things she didnt have to say
          and she'll say um again   you know what i mean
          if she has to say um   you know what I mean

that next day
i twisted my school of engineering corporate afro
into little starter dreads
my head was a roosevelt WPA replanted forest in the great northwest

me and angry sister x
would read our poems over breakfast
they were fresh
smelt of incense and just crushed hummus

garbanzo beans are the seeds of freedom
i couldnt wait till my dreads tickled the tips of my ears

we figured going to hear this established poet
might promote our hair growth

a poet whose description under his picture read

the author is a demolitions expert an accomplished marksman
        philosopher
black belt voodoo witch doctor lobbyist who lives in a thatch hut in
        rwanda
and is at present trying to get congress to pass the james bond act
law that permits black people to drink martinis with a straight face
and to kill white folks with impunity

with his revolutionary tomes
in her purse
folded in my back pocket

we sat and listened in a white church

but this poet had on a pressed starched collared shirt
i kept looking back at his picture
                is cuz the same motherfucker
                is this the same nigga

he was missing
his mutton chop hate whitey side burns
and read long monotone poems   that was all right
but they were about elephants in his bedroom
and how he was tryin to get in touch
with his lithuanian roots

twice i saw a white rabbit
stick its head out his left blazer pocket
noticed he had a habit of rubbing
the office boy leather patches on his tweed jacket
whenever he told one of his
intermittent drab adages about where he taught at

after we left we realized he never said black   not once
                                        maybe we'd missed something
             okey doke nigga aint said shit
             white folks laughed at his jokes
             but i wasnt eatin granola   i was lookin for smoke

i want to see some dead blue eyed hoogies or im goin home

who turned the magic fire hose on his dashiki
and turned it into one of them
irish spring soap commercial prep school sweaters

                        bell bottoms to pleated chino khakis
                        platforms to hush puppies

fuck the elephants graveyard
i want to know where does the revolutionary spirit go to die

i want to be one of those withstand any torture tippy top secret solo
jujitsu take two double cyanide suicide tablets revolutionary agents you
can skin me with that rusty bic disposable shaver but i aint gon say shit
hope-to-die negro poets

hell bent on revenge
that force feeds dagwood bumstead triple decker rye bread
kill the peckerhead sandwiches to those starved for the payback

and the crowd be eatin all that shit up too
but i bring my own lunch in a brown paper bag
liverwurst and mustard   doritos   hostess cupcakes

my mouth full yellin
yo wait up   im fixin to get with this revolution
             but i got crazy indigestion

plop plop fizz fizz
oh what a revolution this is

we used to come home on college vacations
pissed n miffed at the system

open the fridge

    there aint no kool-aid
    see mom how fucked up shit is

thats when sylvester come home
fresh out his yellow construction foreman pick-up truck
he'd dust the country music off his dungarees
reshape the chicago in his afro

look at the anger in our teary visined eyes
smell the hurt on our beer drenched breath
and say

revolutionary thrills
without revolutionary skills
will get you killed

the mud on my shoes
the arthritis in your mothers fingers
1000 hours of cosmetology school—
hair weaves jheri curls and cold waves
nigga dont you see self hatred paid for your education

        looks like we made it
        left each other on the way to another love
        looks like we made it

you have the barry manilow live on broadway album
        yo thats the jam   the gonzo hits medley is dope

so what revolutionary classes you take this semester
karate?   no

riflery?   nope
introduction to molotov cocktails zip guns and other easy to assemble
weaponry for the do-it-yourself rebel?   no

what classes did you have
i took gemstones

how you gonna kill the enemy
by blinding em
with the luster of the onyx and gold in your class ring
that sheepskin you want so bad
aint nothin but south african pass
that lets you in and out of they world
lets them know you harmless brainwashed and can roll your r's
rrrrrrrrevoluuution

got mad ran to my room
punched my stuffed bert and ernie dolls in the nose
and turned on the late night news
little kids throwing rocks at tanks

guess i'll never be warrior stock
i've only thrown rocks at the windows
in the abandoned houses on my block
and at the heads of my best friends

dont know how to fight so i write
in elementary school i used to draw a small hill
in each corner of the bottom of the page
then a big hill in the middle
stick figures with machine guns

      i was real good at makin explosions
                  guys would come up to me look over my shoulder
              and say   thats baaad explosion

      thanks dude

stick figures with machine guns
fightin it out till the recess bell rung
and i realize that no one ever won
so i write paper airplane bombs

for kids on mall reconnaissance
shootin spit balls at people they dont know

you suck brssszzzzzz errrrrunnnnggg boom!
im down with this and oh yessss im definitely with that
bidduddududd   blam!

and i got james taylor art garfunkel and paul simon
                              on in the background
singin
dont know nothin bout history
no who
who are you really

im so confused

                              i dont know shit from shinola
                         dont know the shah from the ayatollah
                              dont know coke from pepsi cola

revolution
shhh the revolution is fought when your lover
is at the door
on the way out

gives you a kiss and a side order of hips
wiggle and swivel
and you cant come with it

bodys stiff
emotional overload
playin ditch with the process of change

the little rascal submits

learn that poem   learn that poem

bill are you ready to recite the piece

tears streaming down my face
i say yes teacher

way upon a hill
i spy a little daffodil

Quote Unquote

i am telling you white people . . .
are evil

        how can you say that
        your own mother is white

then dont you think
i should know
what im talking about

Tap Tap on Africa

listen to this old soul sufferin
from rheumatic post-disco fever
my unbuffered bones groan and whine
my juked joints lock and pop

i usta *dance dance dance*

now the weekend chizzem-bop has stopped
ive developed this cough
every day is a day off

i usta count steps   *left right left   kick ball change*

today i sip kaopectate and calculate
the lost opportunity costs
of being uh yessir boss american after party african

you got any aspirin
i get these excedrin harriet tubman headaches n pains

who said shit bout bein sane

rub some ben-gay into my lump
punch-drunk and hunchbacked
from lifetimes of limbo dancin
under the new worlds tolls

poll taxes
and turnstiles

got any tylenol
im not
feelin very poetic
angina of the mind my brain is stalled i feel so behind

yesterday while runnin late for the late freight

i had a historical backstroke
that paralyzed my right side

now my eye droops
my cheek sags
the corners of my lips clap n drag
and everytime a young african whippersnapper
starts braggin that jesus was black

i have these
non-believer milk of magnesia seizures
where i flop around on the floor

                                    blabberin
                                    about the caucasian dark ages
                                    when white folks lived in caves

in this trance
my grandmarnier liquored lips
speak in ancient tongues
choking gurglin bits of summer sanskrit

yearround spasms
shake the bodylocked arms of my family tree
            droppin leaves of swahili

        that with afro-centric photosynthesis
                                    turn from
                                    black to blackest
                                    before they hit
                                    the streets of genesis

myth

did you say myth

no no i said *miss*
see whenever i talk about africa
i lisp

i meant to say miss
as in
your original man is a woman   so whos been hyp no tized

look into my
star lit hollywood nigger in motion picture eyes

eyes that boogedy boogedy bulge
with watermelon hieroglyphs

spirals
bird profiles
squiggly lined graffiti poems on the feet of the sphinx
what does it mean
i dont know but the rhyme scheme was

                    snake
                    snake
                    zigzag
                    ibis

figures that if liz taylor is cleopatra
a thousand years from now
marilyn monroe will look like whoopi goldberg in ghost

just supposin that i
really could talk to the dead
i would *roll over beethoven*
say wuddup g
and heed go

                    no symphony no. 4 should be in b flat

that would make chuck berry
a rock n roll prophet with a process
or at least a method to the madness

to the chronic i want a cadillac coup de ville
mental illness of little boy / little girl blu-black
horner harmonica   painted into a corner
                    tryin to play the songs
                    on the instructions in the box
never knew *on top of old smokey*
was so complicated

  the man at the store said
  all i had to do
  was put the mouth organ to my heart
  he said   ancestry is a hard disk
  and like doctor seuss's elephant in horton hears a who
                                        your soul never forgets

i said what i meant
an i meant what i said
the genetic code is faithful 100% percent

so i sit at home
cross-legged on the carpet
moanin   constantly rockin
mesmerized that the only beat i can keep
is the steady knock of my head against the wall

the forehead as mallet
the wall as gong

gong
time for tea
gong
time for prayer
gong

time to plead
gong
whens somebody gonna give the drummer some

problem iz
after these fits
i cant remember shit

i know theres a need for theory
                              epistemology
                              and new deeds to greek philosophy

but i still want
time to party   go-plato go-plato

so i ask god to bless
this all-purpose definition of afro-centrism

                    think of the world
                    as a rubiks cube

a game of plastic plate tectonics
where the object
                 is continental segregation

the challenge is to put each color onna different side

     the greens over here
                         the yellows
                         over there
                         blues next to the red knuckleheads
                         and the whites on top

but no matter
             how much you twist n turn
        no matter

                    what magic words you say   *hocus pocus*
                                               roota voota voo
                                               alakazam

the colors is still
every goddamn which-a-way

so afro-centrism
solves the problem
by spray paintin the whole thing black

Desert Boots

peace rallyin around
aint even heard the body count

and the part i cant figure out
is what everybodys smilin about

this w.h.a.m.
           a w.h.a.m. is what collette calls
           a white honky american male
           well i put in the honky part

anyways this w.h.a.m.
with a bullhorn and an opinion

is yellin about burnin babies in kuwait
and people yell back peace
and start smilin hug their mates patchin up their relationships

i dont get it he said burnin babies

look up and another w.h.a.m. speech

this time tom is tying the newspaper strike to holy jihad with a simple

           . . . and these are the same motherfuckers . . .

im down with the unions but i dont get the connection

           the connection is that
           . . . these are the same motherfuckers . . .

but

           . . . these are the same motherfuckers . . .

ecofeminists against bullshit
                . . . and these are the same motherfuckers . . .

african pacifists
                . . . and these are the same motherfuckers . . .

everyone was gettin much dap
sos i decided to piggy back
on this anti-aircraft semipro iraq flac
opened my trap
and said

im against the war and fact is i need some new sneakers
no one was with me
                till i said

                . . . and these are the same motherfuckers . . .
and the crowd said peace

what do we want!   NEW SHOES   when do we want it!   NOW

what do we want!   PEACE   when do we want it!   NOW

and these is the same motherfuckers who only say peace when
america is at war
most of the time its we this and we that
they could give less than a fuck about me

but today they shakin my hand
talkin about
brothermanbrothermanbrotherman

when we
breathe peace and exhale freedom

you leave the scene
its   yo check you out later

be safe   take care   nice to meet you   peace

burnin candles
burnin flags
burnin bridges

and so far these chants
aint stopped anything
but traffic

          hey hey! ho ho!
          whatever i dont like has got to go!

dont sleep on peace
but give it time
to march past moments of silence
that drag it on bleedin knees through whatever suits who-so-evers needs

Daryl Patterson and Bugs Bunny's
Black Nationalist Cheerleading Camp

Ricka Rocka! Ricka Rocka!
Sis Boom Ba!
Malcolm X! Malcolm X!
Rah! Rah! Rah!

What a Pity, What a Shame

went to hear marion williams
sing the gospel yesterday

       she was singin so hard

              i almost slipped up
                and let jesus into my heart

Two Pink Dots? You Positive?

make a life.   take a life.
that's what they say, that's how they think.
its a well-rehearsed macho thought process
a litany of hand-me-down pocket pool epiphanies
followed by: *word   right, right   you know it*

me and my bloated belly float by and still they wink.
then without askin,
                          they rub
                     my summer stomach *lil nigga must be sleep, yo*

steve, reece, and supreme
call themselves full house,
becuz they believe they
                three kings with a pair of queens each

its high stakes playing poker with players
who can make   *hello, how you doin'?*   sound like a threat
                girl you better speak

and i ante up with,
what's going on?

maxin   chillin
damn these motherfuckers must barely move   *what's new?*

jus coolin

sometime a nigga stick his neck out
from the peer group n say sumpthin stupid

wish i could have a baby

scuse me?   while you so pseudo-delirious
then you had better say i wish i could have periods.
hushed that madness right the fuck up.

but right then   i knew
i was carryin
a boy

                         i could feel him want to get out
                         hang with the crowd
                         but he couldnt

      so he leaned back
                put one foot on my uterus
                pulled pants he didnt have down to the crack of his ass
                tilted his baseball cap

barely into his third trimester
and the little squirt was already down wid O.P.P.
every other day
after breast feeding,
i make sure he sees the stretch marks
from my crotch to the watch he wants for his birthday.

                    he loves mickey mouse
                    askin company to slap his chubby hands
                    gimme four man, gimme four

my shit
was so ripped up . . . stitches

remember
             that facilitator
                              at Teen-age Mothers at Risk?

nerve to show me pictures of her afterbirth.

"Oh no girl, pregnancy is worth it.

Here is Kevin's placenta
on the beach in Jamaica . . .

Here's the umbilical cord eating cotton candy at Disneyworld . . ."

thought she was teasing me.
i aint never been on a vacation in my life,
thought her job was to make things easier.

shouldnt have quit though,
i was unprepared.   no prenatal care.

next thing i know   im havin contractions in the cab

thought i was going to die
but i played the cool role
thought you got to the hospital
and dropped the load
                              nope
asked the doctor,
how long is this thisthis this labor business?

he said it could last all day and thats when i proceeded to go crazy.

i got real hot.   took off my smock and just started starin at the clock.

barry, my nigga, stopped lookin at the nurses then.
say you naked baby, put your things back on.
put that man in a headlock and together we addressed the doctor

you mean i gotta go all the way around?
        i gotta go all the way around?

look baby they talkin about
                          one
                              two
                                  three
                              four
                          five
now i know what they mean by
a race against time.

        it wuz mothers on your marks
        get set   and i jetted

ran down the hall
butt naked
big belly shakin,

started ravin   take this baby, get this motherfucker out now.

and the hospital said in that singsong voice
as if i was a kid in for a tonsillectomy

Mi-i-ss, y-y-your n-n-o-t di-a-lated.
fuck it then c-section   scalpel get a goddamn scalpel   STAT
                    mudderfuckah   STAT,
                    i watch doogie howser   STAT.

barry's hands danced all over my skin.
babes please . . . babes please calm down.

                          nigga shut up

doctors were like "Sir is your wife on drugs?"
                "She's on drugs. You cannot have this baby here."
the nurses they was Jamaican yknow
sounded like the I Threes.

moanah you must calm down
the baby moanah the baby

but i didn't feel irie   i felt irate

the doctors said
                "Miss you not ready for no baby"

                well its too late now, aint it?
i didnt ask for this baby i dont want this kid i didnt ask for this baby
                                    i dont want this kid

the I Threes their hands clasped in sympathy shimmied up to me
shakin their tambourines

moanah you must calm down
the baby . . .
the baby, the baby will get a disease

i dont care

remember lamaze   breathe baby just breathe

you should have seen me,
went into my nude marylou retton.

            you dont see too many gymnasts with big hips,
            but i was doin a flip flop n somersault floor routine
            finally some orderlies got to me
            doctor gave me an enema said i would feel better.

and I did a little bit
went to the toilet
and all of a sudden another pain hit
and i shot up
still shittin

left a hansel and gretel trail of diarrhea
from triage
                    to the maternity ward
                                        and all over the lounge
got up on the couch
and announced i want this baby out of me now

barry started lookin to the other men for help
and all they could say
                    was *i'm glad thats not my wife*

babes babes what about lamaze?
maybe if we put a little water on your lips

thats when i knew the situation was desperate
so i dropped to the ground face first
and tried to push the baby out.

                              pressed my distended stomach
                              against that cold tile

the nurses:
moanah you gwine ta kill the baby moanah

and blam the baby started comin out
got on the gurney and when he was out i felt fine

100 cc of demerol
and two days later
i woke to the entire hospital staff
sayin miss you better not have no more kids
and didnt none of them laugh neither

post partum depression
wouldnt touch or feed the kid
hated it

my boyfriend had to take care of him for two weeks

it was a mess
me and the baby cryin
barry was walkin in circles sayin,
> *the bigger the headache the bigger the pill*
> *the bigger the headache the bigger the pill*

but now i love my child
wont let nobody touch him
least of all those lazy niggas who say   *wish i could have a baby*

and for some reason when i walk the street
and the men say hi
i no longer feel as if i have to speak

Mickey Mouse Build a House

don't you ever feel
like in the game of life

you was the last motherfucker to say

NOT IT

Independent Study

everydays homecoming at sidewalk university / harlem campus

shreds of yellow newspaper
instead of tree leaves
tumble thru broken fields of glass
to quiet autumn touchdowns

if cat stevens
lived in harlem
he wouldnt have to ask *where do the children play*
they play in the streets
two-hand touch
purple and green nerf spirals
three completes first
take two steps turn around

i was open on that last play
the only thing open was your nose
you just stay back and block

       sidewalk chickenhawks
       begin to line the parade route

       hot dogs sauerkraut

the brownstone stoops are grandstand pigeon coops
a place to coo n schmooz the harlem blues
a wc handy place to wait for the chickens to come home to roost
remember when x said that about kennedy
at temple 7

       now theres a rhode island red sittin on his chest
       singin fight songs at the high jumpin sun

i guess thats what happens
when you strut n buck
the pecking order

standing behind invisible police barricades
the crowds wave

as the drop tops
coast by

      prize winning floats
      metallic *im drivin you not* boasts

and you know niggas be scopin
heads out the windows
pick up lines and oldies
on harlem days that *float   float on*

        aquarius   and my name is ralph . . .
           now i like a woman
           who loves her freedom

the nigger please cheerleaders laugh
at this old straitjacket rap
these new age african harriet houdinis
with comeback lines like bobbipins
free themselves from the claptrap

cartwheels and handsprings
propel them awwwwww beepbeep   down the street

sometimes bullshit walks
carryin a box   *naw baby for real   my carz in the shop*
then the love lyrics drop

libra   *and my name is charles   now i like a woman whos quiet*
        a woman who carries herself like mrs. universe

my fathers name is charles
and my mother is quiet

but he didnt like her cause she carried
herself like herself

thru the balloonless halftimes between riots
uprisings when neighborhood drill teams
marched thru cannon smoke

throwin flaming twirling molotov batons
way up in the air
then watched them hit the ground
crazy   i aint catchin shit

a hunchedback drum major
highsteps over the ashes
blowin the whistle on the revolution

its the homecoming queens
day off from burger king
a rest from the constant *push up* codas

I'LL TAKE AN ORANGE SODA   what size
BOUT YOUR SIZE   that be about a medium

she rides on the hood
of a red on red gypsy cab
naugahyde interior
her long legs crimp styles

if you spliced speaker wires
to the lonely pop pop pops of hearts

cancer and my name is larry

the trip light sparks
in the mack daddies eyes
would walk right up to the side of her ride

grab the door handles
dapper dan secret service agent style
hoping to protect her from the whispering bullets of jive
thanks   but she got a bulletproof vest called pride
her bald headed driver smiles

his liver wrapped
in a brown paper bag
neil diamond on the radio
a mid-term in community college intro to eastern religion on his mind
the bhagavad gita on his lap
and aint harlem just like the parade of ants

Big Bowls of Cereal

with absolutely no regrets
i spent the summer of my discontent
in the corner arcade

bent over the pinball machine
nine extra balls and a line of niggas
                         sucking they teeth
                              waitin for me to get off

       the change guy thinks i am a genius
       my high scores blink on the backglass
       of every video game ever made

                    but my real teenage wasteland claim to fame
                    is that every fall i get teased and taunted
                    for being the dumbest kid in gifted class

the ultimate idiot savant
i can recite Immanuel Kants *Critique of Pure Reason*
but i cant tell you what "categorical imperative" means

       all his grief
       cause during an iq test
       i strung a string of beads
       tossed around some proverbs

   when the proctor said
   a stitch in time saves nine
   i didnt ask nine what   i simply nodded my head   yes   that maxim
    is the shit

you should have heard me make up the meanings for the long words
astutely point out the absurd

if the sun sets in the west
how can a tree cast a shadow in that direction

i can give you the day of the week and the weather
for any date in history

the crucifixion? it was a friday hazy partly cloudy with easterly winds

supposedly got a head on my shoulders
but nobody asks me
what i think
only what i know
which isnt much
            dont seem to have the scholastic touch

D in trig
slept through college prep

        flunked chem
        by letting the rules slide
        and pass me by

    never did memorize all the elements
    just sat there
    an inert black gas
    chemically unreactive to the difference between density and mass

i was cool with the conversion from celsius to fahrenheit
but then cuz started talkin about water was thicker than ice
and i wuz like   right

may i be excused from the atomic table

Krypton
Xenon
Neon   everyone knows im just a C minus peon
            with the dirtiest workstation

unable to balance the electrons in this nuclear age equation
and according to my calculations

                ive come of age
                in an age
                where age aint nothing but a number

ever since i was ten
i aint never been nothin but a man

                        yes ma'ams calloused hands
                        whats happenin little man

aging faster than a vampire
with a stake in its heart

terrible two
teething on the universe
already old enough
to know better
                    before i had ever written a love letter
                    if someones older sister
                    called my poker faced
                                    peach fuzz
                                        sexual bluff
                    and asked me how old i was
                    i knew to say that i was always   old enough

i am old
old enough to remember shag carpeting
and the matted down path that went from the front door straight to
    the bathroom

old enough to remember slow gliding fives on the black hand side
   hip huggers
                  'n punch bugs 'n free love

old enough to remember when The Gap
was the bogus clothing equivalent of Radio Shack

old enough to know that not knowing whats right
has made me unsure nervous
the type of cat who needs instant feedback

i feel like im always on tv and dont know what to do with my hands
with every "yo and hello"
my hands move around uncontrollably
the ginsu knives of my mind
slicing and dicing life down to julienne potato size
i feel like i must act now

im a $19.95 plus shipping and handling type nigga
who everytime he makes a point
taps you on your joints   shoulder   knee
punctuates his speech with rhetorical self-esteem
know whut um sayin
just to see if you're listenin
know whut um sayin

periodically i kick sonic *bust it booms*
not to see if you're moved
but just so it feels like im groovin

so buss it boom

thats me   an ungroomed
                  black boy polaroid
                        underdeveloped grapevine double print of my dad

being driven mad by my grandmother
this ex-flapper draggin me to the mall
cause she went through my stuff
and decided i didnt have enough draws

bussit boom
fruit-a-looms

grandma be crazy cruisin
you be behind her
wunderin *what the fuck is she doin?*

                in the fast lane
                tailgatin time
                trying to make the conversation last

known her all my life
still hard to break the ice

            be talkin to her all loud
        little red riding hood riding shotgun
          suspicious of the wolf
    hey grandma! what mighty big eyes for you ta have!

been drivin these streets for years
now she pretends like she cant see
nose pressed against the windshield
asking directions eyes peeled for some attention

turn signal on for the past five intersections
then she abruptly cuts you off
and wheels that brown buick skylark into the wrong parking lot
her plastic bracelets
click clack
clank 'n clinkin
down crinkly charles chestnutt

high hinkdy yellow forearm flab
wiggling through an illegal u-turn into oncoming traffic

hey grandma!

the fact that i need some clothes
to her is the most important thing in the world
unjam my nineteen year old knees from the glove compartment
squeeze out the front seat
on my way to what god willing will be my last back-to-school sale

"youll like nordstroms they have a good selection"
walkin to the mens section
department store erection
from thinkin about past sins
me my friends and the young miss mannequins

"boy you get everything you need"   ok grandma

pickin through the bargain bin
tryin to find something she thinks is nice
something thats not too expensive
and i could bear to wear at least twice

she dont play the radio
on our sunday drives
our once-a-year september shopping spree
afraid that i'll get mad
and throw a tantrum
now that im kind of curious about what she listens to
she dont play the radio

i miss the
long distance staticky baritone shortwave gospel gibberish
outta nashville
the Peaceway Temple's founder and overseer Prophet Omega
and now todays program

Friends seen 'n unseen
people dat are ridin' 'long in their automobeels
peeppll that are sittin' at the table
i greet you with the holy word peace
fo' with my intimate mind i think constructively
fo' yo' minds are my min' and my min' is yo' min
and imuh sendin' out my christ mind to you you 'n you

now grandma just hum
change lanes for no reason
askin me when im going to church
i slurp the last of my vanilla shake
watching the stop lights go by

i dont know grandma im just tryin to get over
getting over usta mean your soul crossing into heaven
   not getting over the hump
      or getting over on some punk

    i just cant get into
       munchin dry fish and bread
          free lunch sandwiches on the beach with jesus

         and if he had really turned water into wine
          my whole neighborhood be on line

now every year a bit before christmas
i see jesus reincarnated in the theater district
showin off his double dealin three card monte
mr magician parlor tricks
whistlin *how i got over*

         fleecin the meek
         spittin and playin the unhip for vics
         one eye out for the police

here come one now
shepherd of sheep
blowin a plastic shofar

"ease up cuz"
the game disappears
the playing table
flops into cardboard box litter
the apostle shills and stick men hit it
mesh into the crowd
walkin a little quicker step than everyone else
get outta dodge the pedestrians pep

                 meet you at the spot   go for self   yep   bet

tony toi's sister nica's boyfriend
showed me the tricks
in a challenge of wits
street savvy vs. booksmarts

right at the start
he bent the corner of the red card
i thought to myself thats it
another stupid ghetto nigga done slipped

                los angeles summer vacation misdirection
          your eyes stuck on the disfigured suicide king of hearts
       the quickness in his wrists   the spiel   the con mans diss

you a straight A nigga
blam goddamn dumb ass motherfucker
this one and that is black
the red and you get paid
pick the correct shit

threw a dollar on the coach
and my dog-eared sure fired winner
was the nine of spades listenin to pot call the kettle names

lets go again run it back black
academically enriched   pitchin a fit
but now who's gettin over?   who's schoolin who?

pardon me   who is gettin over on whom

my english teacher says never use the word get

but only other synonym comes to mind is take
    what about receive?
    i dont never get nothing that way
    if i dont take it i wont get it
    well dont use get in your writing understand?   yeah i get you

get busy
get back
get taken   *get* took off   i *got* mines you *get* yours

punks get got in the age of hiphop
the trained eye
can spot the *spots*
i spy . . . some proper talkin american polka dots

               houseparty party-mix misfits
         wallflower wild irish red-light roses
                  tryin to be different

  slow dancin with after-images of a kind   of nigga   that doesnt exist

reluctant hominy grit homonyms
watchin the sweat on the windows drip
come monday they
refuse to strip in gym
prefer to play tetherball
four square and hopscotch
on rainy days they play charades with race

—sounds like—
a high school fake monty python british accent

where you from old chap, london?   naw watts

would be kings and queens of scots
shankin dreams of crippled crabs sleep in a barrel
obsessive compulsive
washin yo hands of the blood
one drop rule and my cup runneth over
Out, damned spot! Out, I say! Niggas will be niggas!
One—two—why then, then 'tis time to do 't.
Niggers and flies I do despise, the more I hate niggers the more I like
     flies
Hell is murky.

the first budget cut is the deepest
after they got rid of CETA
i needed a summer job

i could be a geologist
learn about rocks
down at my uncles spot
but on second thought if the cops came   and the spot got hot
i would be all nervous   and uh lil nigga like me be in the way 'n shit

buss it boom

when raymond heard that i didnt get the gig
he introduced his bestfriend hector to uncle rick

his résumé was the look on his face
with a handshake
whatever little kid hector had left in him evaporated
ruddy cheeked innocence blanched into a pale myth of a man
for the next week all he could say was
          playin for keeps, my brother playin for keeps

as you seek so shall you reap
ghetto peepshow
college radio out of long beach

        you hip to the underground scene
        that nigga fat joe
        going toe to toe with the whole world
        spraying the mike with saliva
        at 2:30 on a thursday night friday morning

up late doin my biology homework

gregor mendel genetic hybridization
i got the blue eye brown eye snow peas dominant genes in pod
    permutations down
and no one had to tell a lonely nigga like me
about self pollination

grandmas still up in the front room
watching telemundo
say boy   that biology book explain why
        on these latin american *novelas*
        all the men got black hair and shades
        and all the women are blond love slaves
mendel dont explain that

        or if poverty is hereditary
        grandma brush some dust from the tv screen
        with the flat of her hand

i ask her how come she and ms. rudolph didnt do windows
she said "cause people can see you doin windows"

you watchin this grandma
"no" (if i ask she aint watchin)
turn the channel   mick jagger singin satisfaction

whos that   rolling stones   as in the papa was   naw as in gathering
    no moss
let me tell you bout satisfaction
in 1938 after years of hearing the white paddies
chant *nigger nigger never die, black face shiny eyed*

     my father and his partner
     came home from the second louis / schmeling fight
     wonderment and pride
     laid his hat down
     did that male side to side jimmy stewart thing to loosen his
       tie

sayin   joe louis hit that man so hard
       schmeling landed on the ropes
       and started screaming aaaaahhhh

           screamed till his corner men
           came and hugged him

he say thats satisfaction
he say thats the only time he ever heard a white man scream   for real

sometimes at night
i can hear pushcart sam
the ghetto town crier
yellin at shadows
the black behind drawn curtains
it's three o clock and everything is fucked up

his left rear shopping cart wheel
wiggles wobbles and squeaks but gets no grease
every few feet it locks and drags
leaving skid marks on the linoleum sidewalks
the earth is an open mall and this city aint nothing but aisle 4
attention all k-mart shoppers

on sundays sam sits on a faded fallen vacant lot refrigerator
sifting through food coupons
looking for 25 cent off pork 'n beans
playin with a tarnished brass mouthpiece
that seems to fit in the louis armstrong crease in his lips

      sam stands and works his fingers
      over the plungers of an air-trumpet
      tattered pin striped suit
      yankee baseball hat as mute

a recycled miles davis anadizin the ghetto in silent aluminum blue tunes?
or gabriel in pork pie hat

      just like a nigga angel runnin late for work
        blowin his horn after the rapture is over

every once in a while
i see the winged spirits of niggas past raise out the rubble
doppel gangbangin ghosts of john henry
urban zeitgeist who fought and died lost and exhausted
from diggin tunnels of love
smith and wesson hammerin against the steam engined deus ex machina
thru stone mountains and neo-conservative molehills

folkloric heart attacks   bustin caps
eulogize and romanticize the guys on their way to the eternal haps

bumper to bumper
dead blacks

there go my brother helpin to direct the traffic
tellin fools back the fuck up   step off   step to this
                              step to that

he helped raise me
but grandma couldnt hold him

not much can
and there he stands   no paddle in the sidecreek to the main stream

babblin and braggin how his is the last face lotsa niggas've seen

as he runs down a who's who in the neighborhood yearbook

see that kid over there who passed
by and waved a shy little hi
thats eric thompson
rahway class of '89
rifle club   varsity B and E team
sergeant at arms for the society of double muslims
ambition—"*I want to fuck the world, put my dick in the earth.*"

for what its worth
nigga owe me fifteen hundred dollars

wuddup mutherfuckah?
when the clock rings
it rings hard

my brother has left niggas in backyards
has left niggas under some dirt

i suppose if i called up my brother said murder that nigguh
drag him to his front door

buss it boom
he do it

sometimes you have to put a mutherfucker in check
mutherfucker do wrong

you make your opening move
walk past a fool nonchalant   pull his card   take his pawn *en passant*

pin the kid in
with palms on the wall boris spassky grandmaster flash attack strategy

was that you who was fucken wid my cousin?

if he castles with denial

naw that wasnt me

    then you go straight to the end game
    fuck with his brain
    move his loved ones to Qe8

dont you live on straight street apt 4G
digits is 555-2468 who do we appreciate
and aint that your pop
be playin the numbers at the spot near the cab stand
wear a green fedora   tilted to the left side monday thru saturday
to the right sunday
thought so
              checkmate

forever playin the mindgame

the other day in psychology
while they was talkin about the oedipus and electra complexes
i was skimmin ahead
looking at the pictures

              figurin that since i was from a broken home
              these psychosexual stages didnt apply to me
              i wasnt obsessed with no feces

    though i might be orally fixated
i sucked my thumb to slumber up until my fourteenth summer

wonder how im gonna grow up
both your parents on drugs
realistic dreamscape not much food on my plate

house is a shooting gallery

on page 98
i came across this skinny scrawny wirebrush bristle haired little monkey
clinging to its bogus man made surrogate mother
big red taillight eyes
a wire torso and pacifiers for breasts

no warmth no affection

i know some mothers like that

my parents were like african voodoo dolls
that their own suicidal spirits stuck syringes in

> poison darts
> and hat pins dipped in
> liquid coping mechanisms

i used to play connect the dots with the pock marks and scars
on my daddys arms

niggas useta tell jokes about my mother
i just lose it

> *nigga, your mother so stupid*
> *when she gets on the elevator and wants to go to the fourth floor*
> *she press two twice*

i just start cryin
dry my eyes
steady lyin bout my pops
whats my father do? oh he's in europe shootin hoops

time for young mens group

      those long winded nationalistic filibusters on culture
      cryptic muslim brothers the acidic citrus fruit of islam
      blacker than johnny cash in gloves and a ski mask

and tellin us how we should live our lives

    . . . and you fellas should be looking for a wife
      that is 7 years your junior
      half past a monkeys ass and a quarter to his balls . . .

rocky watch me pull a rabbit outta my hat
pressin up my sleeves presto!

no no anything but that
not the syllaballistic linguistic bullwinkle bullshit   please no

       b lack bullack be lack beee lack ing   be lacking

                WHAT?

        negro neee grooo   neeee   grooooo neg a tive growth

if this nigga says diaspora forget it we in here for two more hours
well then lets diaspora the fuck outta this motherfuckuh

no notes in my notebook
an at lunchtime me and the homies cook

huddled in the school yard
boys since the swing set
hunched over a tapedeck
rollin our shoulders keepin time with life
and catchin spiritual rec

got a puerto rican coolout
name of billy matos
spend most our time eating french fried potatoes
when we leave its hasta luego
    im hot
como un fuego

oye que pasa
heard about the tabula rasa
but im chalkboard with no chalk
soz i spends my time with the oral jabberwock
tweedledum and tweedledee
there go lewis carroll showin alice his wee wee
"The vorpal blade went snicker-snack!"

fuckin public pool pedophiliac
the big blue meanie starin at
pre-teens in bikinis

"Beware the jabberwock my son!
    The jaws that bite, the claws that catch!"

Who dat?   who dat?   Who dat say who dat, when i say who dat?

    can you show me where he touched you

pssst check my portfolio
like jonas salk
i got the cure for
pimp limpin gangster polio
a vaccine that takes niggas off gods shit list
answers the prayers of wounded hustlers in wheel chairs
wearin 100 dollar sneakers that never touch the sidewalk

        i'll grant you three wishes if you rub my lantern
        oooh   a little to the right

wish i may wish i might first star i see tonight

schmiel schmallzle
fizzle fazzle
still a little kid cause i like to eat razzles
flim flam-a-diddle
no time to quibble
ready set hut take the snap
and run straight up the middle

i aint in it to win it
im just trying to hook up with a crew
be on the periphery
be a back up rapper
an S1W or some shit

be response to they call
a supreme behind diana ross
a pip behind gladys knight
kokomo to joe schmoe

blaa blaa HEY!

yakkity yak gats bats n hats   HOO!

put on my gear and act goofy in the video

not translucent   not see through   not bulletproof
kind of obtuse

opaque

a jittery kid in the national spelling bee
reluctantly leaves a metal chair
cardboard sign dangling and banging on birdlike prepubescent chest
tender nipples

opaque

may i have a definition?
                        vague   dark 'n dull   hard to understand   obscure

may i have the origin?
middle english

that figures   what   *nothing may i have an alternate pronunciation?*

oh pah queue

can you use the word in a sentence?

when asked to put a check in the box marked race
the respondent chose   opaque (non-hispanic)

opaque   O-P-A-Q-U-E   opaque

wearin the subway bus
public transportation deadpan ghetto face
the educated sympathetic liberal doesnt understand
i want to be ralph ellisons invisible man
peek-a-boo i see you
run the jewels

thats what i like about black people they fuck with the rules

we usta play marco polo
when the kid who couldnt swim was it . . .
ok you guys tell me if im going towards the deep end of the pool

marco!   *polo!*   marco!   *polo!*   marco blubblubblubblub

5 10 15 20 25 30 *my cheri amour pretty little girl that i adore* 95 100
ready or not here i come

buster be in the middle of the street
yellin alli alli outs in free
            and when you came out he beat you for beatin him

when buster was it
we hid in obvious places
behind fire hydrants
under the sky
tap tap on your black ass
hidin behind the crab grass

                        twenty horses in a stable one   got   out

now we hide in the library
it be few of us in there
sittin in front of the big metal fan
squeezed in little wooden chairs
it so quiet
no hoodlums
just the mutter of bookworm bums

come february i like watching
the little kids and their parents
excited with annual pride
rush ms. biot

can i help you

you the librarian? i wanna do something on black history
lemme have a book on black history

what part of black history are you interested in

just black history
gimme the goddamn black history book

ms. biot be cursin   waitin on march 1st
you stupid niggas get the fuck outta here

word
word is weak
shhhh quiet down
naw man a messerschmitt take out a P-38 lightning fighter/bomber
you crazy turn the page

the library is our barbershop
we sit around in cutoffs and dirty socks
tellin stories
who got shot
taking odds on who gonna get popped

tell the one about your sister and the jewelry shop

the one when boyfriends amos 'n andy malapropped
through life making secret get rich quick schemes

simonize your watches

american dreamers

        call in mid scalp grease
        hot comb
                        as the world turns
        half dressed

the dream needs a vet
and you better be ready when it gets here

                        or else it pulls you into the car
                        by braids barrettes and screams
                        drives twice around the block
                        speakin old movie criminalese

anna go in there and case the joint
lefty knuckles and mugs
when push comes to shove
what you wont do, do for love

you would think a store in the middle of the valley
fifty yards from a freeway on ramp
would be suspicious

if a scared pajama clad light fuzzy blue house shoe wearing ashy
     legged dried up
tears chubby cheeked black woman pippy longstocking pickaninny
     braids on one side
the other newly fried untied and electrified came ten feet into the
     store stared
directly at the jewelry case turned slowly around counting out loud
     the number of
security and sales personnel the steps to the door

sledge hammers broken glass and laughs

she wouldnt take her cut

                    back at the palace with a torn screen door
                    the american dreams mama and her sister
                    sit on the sofa throne
                    sartres' harpies reclined in repose
                    in the kingdom of flies   lay-away and payments
                    counting the take

     child you better take some
     shoot you earned it
     take a chain or somethin
     can you turn up the stereo

ms. biot sees that we've stopped reading
readies to leave
she gives us whatever books we wuz looking at

these are due in two weeks
did i tell you that im psychic
paul   ronald   jamal   you all gonna be lawyers doctors
whatever it is you want
apart from playin ball

another mindgame but we bite
you aint psychic

think of a number between   1 and 9   you got it?
now multiply that number by nine   you got it?
now if its double digits add them up
subtract five from the total

now take that number and replace it with the corresponding letter
    of the alphabet

if its 1 thats an A, if its 2 thats a B, and so on
now think of a country that begins with your letter
now take the second letter of that country and think of an animal
that starts with that letter
now think of the color of that animal

you thinkin of a gray elephant right
how she know
                        naw fool i had a black emu
                            i had a brown elk

grandma
i dont want to die
like some poached animal in the serengeti
a bushman in the kalahari

tuned into radio free europe
listenin to the Prophet Omega

*The Shipp Moving Co. who is located on Old Lexington city highway.
They been in bidness since 19 and 54 and they specialize in movin fahn
furniture, yo' furniture which is fine furniture . . . now fo a courtesy
move uh quick move or a right now move then call Shipp Movin' got
menz ovah dere who are very courtesy an unnerstandin' and don't mind
tryin' to satisfy you the customent. The company give you an
estimatation they don't charge you any extra fo' dat and if the company
move you they don't charge you extra for a heavy piece, uh heavier piece
and they got some beautiful girls ovah dere doin' the packin' 'n unpackin'
now this cost you extra. But what is a little extra for safety ssss? Yo'
glasses don't be broken. Yo' silverware wrapped nice . . . the very things in
which you treasure wrapped and unwrapped took down and put up. Now
that's the Shipp Movin' Co., you may call them at 242-5381 thats
243-5381, 242-5381*

think i'll go to school
get me some of that United Negro College Fund money lou rawls
and that marathon parade of fading hollywood stars
raise every holiday

fool, what you gonna take up in college?
space

Stall Me Out

why you   no rhythm

afraid of women asexual pseudo intellectual
bald mt. fuji shaped head

          no booty havin   big nose
     size 13 feet   pigeon toed crook footed

taco bell burrito supreme eatin
          day dreamin

                              no jump shot   cant dunk
comic book readin
nutrition needin

knock kneed sap sucker
non drivin
                         anti fashion
          constantly depressed   clumsy no money mutherfucker

                         take your weak ass poems
                         and go back to los angeles

*Paul Beatty was born in L.A.
and currently lives in New York City.*

PENGUIN POETS